GOING
Green

David and Patricia Armentrout

Rourke
Publishing LLC
Vero Beach, Florida 32964

www.rourkepublishing.com

PHOTO CREDITS: © Viktoriya Yatskina: Title Page; © Honda Media: page 4 top, 29 bottom; © Vadim Kozlovsky: page 4 bottom; © Brandon Alms: page 5; © Brittany Carter Courville: page 9; © tomos3: page 9 top; © Terrance Emerson: page 9 bottom; © Siemens: page 11; © edge69: page 11 inset; © Tony Tremblay: page 13; © Armentrout: page 15 inset; © Alexander Hafemann: page 15; © Blackred: page 16 inset; © Richard Schmidt-Zuper: page 16, 17; © Jaap Hart: page 19; © Varina and Jay Patel: page 21; © Eric Foltz: page 23 top; © Cheryl Graham: page 23 bottom: © Archives: page 24; © Oralleff: page 25; Elena Elisseeva: page 27; © Steve Dibblee: page 28; © Andrew Soloyev: page 29 top; © Matej Pribelsky: page 31; © Gretar Ivarsson: page 31 inset; © Majoros Laszlo: page 32, 33; © wsfurlan: page 35; © Yinyang: page 36; © General Motors/Matthew Staver: page 37; © Rob Marmion: page 38; © Jani Bryson: page 39; © Nancy Louie: page 41; © Mike Clarke: page 42; © Kristin Smith: page 43; © Skip ODonnell: page 45; © Julien Grondin: page 45 background

Edited by Kelli Hicks

Cover design by Nicky Stratford, bdpublishing.com
Interior design by Teri Intzegian

Library of Congress Cataloging-in-Publication Data

Armentrout, David, 1962-
  Going green / David and Patricia Armentrout.
    p. cm. -- (Let's explore global energy)
  ISBN 978-1-60472-323-6
  1. Power resources--Juvenile literature. 2. Energy conservation--Juvenile literature. I. Armentrout, Patricia, 1960- II. Title.
  TJ163.23.A76 2009
  333.72--dc22

                              2008025137

Printed in the USA

CG/CG

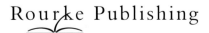

Rourke Publishing

www.rourkepublishing.com – rourke@rourkepublishing.com
Post Office Box 3328. Vero Beach. FL 32964

Table of Contents

CHAPTER ONE

What does Going Green mean?

Most products we buy come in packages, and packaging ends up in landfills. We produce many of the things we use in factories, and most factories burn fuels that pollute the air. Going green means improving the way we produce, buy, use, and throw away products. It means contributing less to air pollution and to landfills. Going green means doing things in ways that are friendly to the environment.

How can we be friendly to the environment? We can start by using more green energy. Using green energy does little, if any, harm to the environment.

Fuel for Thought

Other terms for green energy are alternative, clean, and renewable energy.

CHAPTER TWO

Global Energies

Renewable Energy

SOLAR ENERGY

- Heat and light energy from the Sun
- Renews day after day as the Sun shines

WIND ENERGY

- Motion energy from the wind
- Renews day after day as the wind blows

HYDROPOWER ENERGY

- Energy from moving water
- Renews day after day in waves and flowing rivers

GEOTHERMAL ENERGY

- Heat and steam energy beneath the earth's surface

BIOMASS ENERGY

- Plant material and animal waste used to generate energy

There are many forms of green energy, the most important of which is the Sun. The Sun is our ultimate energy source; it provides heat and light. Without the Sun, plants and animals could not survive. In addition, many of the green energies you will learn about begin with energy from the Sun.

We meet our energy needs with the sources listed below. However, most of the world's energy comes from nonrenewable sources.

Nonrenewable Energy

COAL
- Solid that takes millions of years to form
- Mined from the earth

OIL
- Liquid that takes millions of years to form
- Pumped from the ground

NATURAL GAS
- Colorless odorless gas that takes millions of years to form
- Pumped from the ground

PROPANE GAS
- Natural gas that becomes a liquid gas at high pressure or at low temperature
- Found with natural gas and oil

NUCLEAR ENERGY
- Stored in atoms-the smallest particles of chemical elements
- Formed using uranium ore which is mined from the earth

CHAPTER THREE

Fossil Fuels and Pollution

We use **fossil fuels**, such as oil and coal, more than any other energy source. We burn them to convert their stored energy to a useable form, heat. Unfortunately, fossil fuels are not green. When burned, they release gases, like carbon dioxide, creating air pollution. Air pollution harms the health of plants and animals.

Most electric power plants burn coal to heat water and produce steam. The steam turns a **turbine**, which powers a **generator**, which produces electricity. Currently, there are about 50,000 coal-burning power plants worldwide. That number is expected to rise 60 percent by 2030. How might the addition of coal-burning power plants affect our health, and the health of our planet?

Fuel for Thought

According to the World Health Organization, air pollution causes 2.4 million deaths each year. Many of the deaths are from lung diseases such as asthma, pneumonia, bronchitis, and emphysema.

CHAPTER FOUR

Greenhouse Gases

Greenhouse gases are gases in the Earth's **atmosphere**. They keep some of the Sun's energy from escaping into space. Greenhouse gases keep Earth warm enough for life to exist. Some of the most powerful and plentiful greenhouse gases are water vapor, carbon dioxide, methane, and ozone. The gases occur naturally, and some are created by human activities. Many people are concerned about the greenhouse gases we create, especially carbon dioxide.

Fuel for Thought

Fossil fuels contain high levels of carbon. We release carbon dioxide when we burn coal, oil, and gasoline made from oil.

Some of the sunlight that hits Earth reflects back into space.

Carbon dioxide and other gases in the atmosphere trap heat, keeping the Earth warm.

Atmosphere

Fuel for Thought 🌱

Trucking, shipping, and flying food from farm to table adds to our carbon dioxide problem. Buying locally grown and raised foods helps reduce greenhouse gases.

For millions of years greenhouse gases remained somewhat constant. When there was a rise or fall in gas levels, time naturally balanced them. Now, we have high levels of carbon dioxide because of all the fossil fuels we burn. Natural processes do not have time to balance the carbon dioxide we release into the atmosphere.

Many researchers agree that high levels of carbon dioxide contribute to global warming. Global warming is the increase of the Earth's average temperature. Replacing some of our fossil fuel energy with green energy can reduce carbon dioxide levels.

CHAPTER FIVE

Solar Power

Solar power is a good alternative energy. Solar power plants produce electricity with the Sun's heat. The power plants collect sunlight with the help of big reflective mirrors. The mirrors direct sunlight to a fluid, which gets very hot. The hot fluid heats water and produces steam without producing carbon dioxide. Then, as in conventional power plants, the steam spins a turbine, which powers a generator.

Solar **thermal** power plants are giant collectors of heat. We can use the same basic concept at home, only smaller, with a solar water heater. Solar water heaters have collection boxes that absorb the Sun's heat. They transfer that heat to water in a storage tank. Solar hot water systems help the environment by reducing the need to burn fossil fuels.

Fuel for Thought

The next time you make tea, don't use the stove to heat water. Instead, place tea bags in a glass jar filled with fresh water. Then, set the jar in direct sunlight and let solar thermal energy do the work.

We use solar cells, called **photovoltaic cells** (PV cells) to produce electricity directly from sunlight. Special materials make up the cells. When sunlight hits the cells, it creates an electric current. PV power plants collect the electricity and send it through power lines, supplying homes and businesses with clean solar power. We can reduce the amount of air pollution we cause if we use more solar energy and less fossil fuel energy.

Fuel for Thought

Can individuals use solar cells? Yes! Some people install solar panels on their house. You can even buy calculators, watches, and many other products that run on solar power.

CHAPTER SIX

Wind Power

Tornados and hurricanes show us how destructive wind is, but wind is also productive. People long ago knew the benefits of wind. They used it to move their sailboats and to spin their windmills. Windmills are machines that do mechanical work for us; everything from crushing grain, to pumping water, to milling wood. No electricity is required, only the power of the wind!

Windmills still operate in many parts of the world. In Australia and Africa, for instance, pump mills are necessary to draw water for humans and livestock. In the Netherlands, pump mills are essential because most of the country lies below sea level. The pump mills stand along polders, which are low-lying sections of land surrounded by dikes. Pump mills drain the polders when they fill with water from rainfall, or from nearby rivers and canals.

Today, wind power is a growing **industry**. Many places around the world use modern wind machines to generate electricity.

Wind farms are electric power plants. They convert clean wind energy to electricity with machines called wind turbines. Wind spins the long blades on a turbine. The spinning blades transfer wind energy to a generator, without producing carbon dioxide. Then, the generator produces electricity.

Wind farms generate electricity worldwide. If we use more wind energy, and less fossil fuel energy, we can reduce the amount of carbon dioxide we release into the air.

Fuel for Thought

Wind farms provide electricity to about 4.5 million American homes.

CHAPTER SEVEN

Water Works!

Hydropower uses the flow of water to do work. When we convert hydropower to electricity, we call it hydroelectric power.

The Grand Coulee Dam in Washington is a hydroelectric power plant. In fact, it is the largest power plant of any kind in the United States. The dam is 5,223 feet (1,586 meters) long. It holds water from the Columbia River in a **reservoir** named Franklin Delano Roosevelt Lake. The power plant has four stations with 33 generators that produce electricity.

Besides providing electricity for eleven western states, Grand Coulee Dam also serves as an outdoor recreation area. Two lakes, hiking trails, a golf course, and guided tours of the dam attract more than a million visitors to Lake Roosevelt National Recreation Area yearly.

Fuel for Thought

Hydroelectricity is the world's most widely used green energy. It supplies about 19 percent of the world's electricity.

Fuel for Thought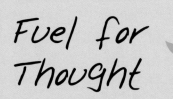

Hoover Dam stands 726 feet (221 meters) tall. Its reservoir is Lake Mead, part of the Lake Mead National Recreational Area.

Many large hydroelectric dams provide electricity to nearby cities. For example, Hoover Dam on the Colorado River generates electricity for areas in Arizona, Nevada, and California.

The Grand Coulee and Hoover Dams rely on gravity. Gravity is a natural force that pulls things down towards the Earth's surface. Engineers build these gravity dams very high. That way the energy in falling water can spin the turbines inside the power plants. If the world used more hydropower electricity, and less fossil fuel electricity, we could reduce air pollution.

Electric generators create electricity at the Hoover power plant.

CHAPTER EIGHT

Hydrogen Power

The Sun, our most powerful energy source, is made up of mostly hydrogen. In fact, all stars consist of hydrogen, the most abundant element in the universe. Hydrogen occurs on Earth, but rarely in its pure form. It is a light gas, which rises in the atmosphere unless it combines with other elements. For example, hydrogen and carbon combine to form hydrocarbons in fossil fuels. Hydrogen also binds with oxygen to form water. In order for us to use hydrogen as a fuel, we first have to separate it from the other elements.

Fuel for Thought

We separate hydrogen from other elements in two ways: by steam reforming fossil fuels, which separates hydrogen from carbon, and by electrolysis with fuel cells, which separates hydrogen from water.

The best way to produce hydrogen, and be friendly to the environment, is to extract it from water. Hydrogen fuel cells use this technology. They produce electricity through a chemical reaction between hydrogen and oxygen. The only by-product is water!

Several carmakers have developed hydrogen-fueled cars. However, most are not ready for sale to the public. Using hydrogen as fuel is not a new idea. NASA has used liquid hydrogen to send rockets into space since the 1970s. Space shuttles use hydrogen fuel cells to power some of their electrical systems. The crew drinks the only by-product, pure water.

Even though hydrogen fuel cell technology has been around for decades, scientists are finding ways to improve fuel cell storage, while reducing production costs. Hydrogen fuel cells have the potential to become a reliable, clean power source.

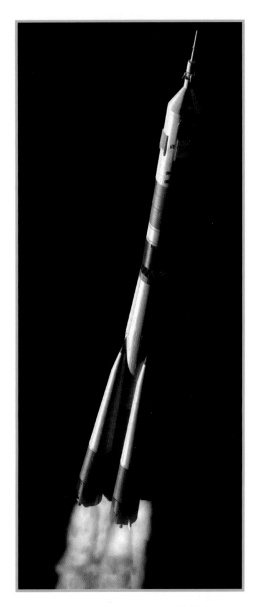

CHAPTER NINE

Geothermal Energy

Geothermal energy comes from deep inside the Earth. It begins in the Earth's core where the temperature is about 12,632 degrees Fahrenheit (7,000 degrees Celsius). The extreme temperature heats rock and water below the surface. Some heat escapes in the form of steam and water through hot springs and geysers. Heat also escapes during volcanic eruptions.

Many countries use geothermal energy to their advantage. Iceland, for instance, pumps hot water from underground and uses it in heating systems. They warm more than 80 percent of their homes with geothermal energy! They also produce about 26 percent of their electricity in geothermal power plants.

The Nesjavellir Geothermal Power Plant in Iceland

Using geothermal energy for hot water is an old practice. Ancient Romans built bathhouses over areas where hot water bubbled up from the ground. Many modern spas and resorts are also near natural geothermal pools.

A geothermal power plant takes the Earth's heat and converts it to electricity. California has the largest group of geothermal power plants in the world. Located north of San Francisco, The Geysers is a power complex. Twenty-two power plants sit four miles above an area of **molten rock**, or magma. The magma heats solid rock and water, creating steam. Drilling rigs bore holes into the earth searching for pockets of steam. Then, pipes transport the steam to turbines above. The Geysers generate clean electric power for 750,000 homes. Using more geothermal energy, and less fossil fuel energy, is another way to reduce air pollution.

CHAPTER TEN

Biomass

Biomass is plant matter and dried animal waste. Plant biomass, such as wood, corn, and sugar cane, is renewable because we can grow it. Animal waste is renewable because, well, animals do what comes naturally.

We burn some biomass and fossil fuels for heat energy. Biomass and fossil fuels have something else in common. Fossil fuels came from plants and animals too. However, those plants and animals lived long ago. In contrast to biomass, fossil fuels take millions of years to form, so they are nonrenewable energies.

Sometimes we don't burn biomass, but burn a fuel made from it. For example, we grow corn and sugar cane for the production of a biofuel called **ethanol**. Burning biomass and biofuels release carbon dioxide just as burning fossil fuels do. However, if we replace the harvested biomass with new plants, they will absorb some of the carbon dioxide during **photosynthesis**.

Photosynthesis is a process by which most plants make their own food by absorbing carbon dioxide and water from the air.

CHAPTER ELEVEN

Making a Difference

Over time, replacing fossil fuels with renewable energies can slow down global warming. But, the responsibility cannot lie on the power companies alone. Individuals can make a big difference.

Fuel for Thought

Did you know the United States government has an agency that protects our health and the health of our environment? It is the Environmental Protection Agency, or EPA. According to the EPA, industry is the number one contributor to greenhouse gases, and transportation is second.

We can do many things on a daily basis that can affect our planet and us in a positive way.

CHAPTER TWELVE

Conserving Electricity

Electricity makes life easier and more comfortable. We use it to power our lights, televisions, computers, and so much more. Conserving electricity is one of the most important things individuals can do to reduce greenhouse gases.

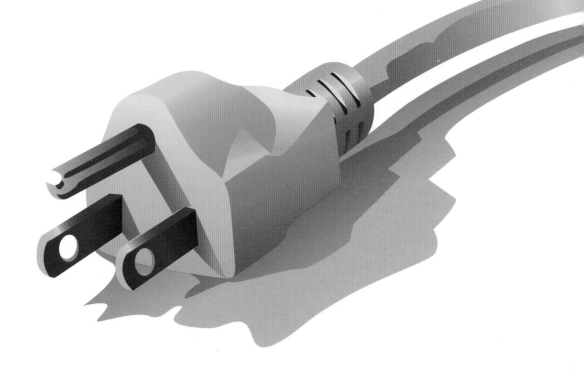

Fuel for Thought

ENERGY STAR is a program of the EPA and the U.S. Department of Energy. These agencies urge people to use energy efficient products to help the environment. According to ENERGY STAR, the average home releases more than twice the amount of greenhouse gases than the average car. That is another good reason to conserve at home!

Conserving electricity and reducing greenhouse gases is easy. One of the best and easiest ways is to turn off unused lights and appliances. Taking advantage of warm sunlight saves energy, and money, too. On a cold winter day, don't turn up the heat. Instead, open the blinds and curtains and let the sunlight in. In the summer, do the opposite. You can reduce the time the air conditioner runs by closing the blinds and curtains. You will be surprised how effective these simple steps can be.

Maybe you are already doing these things. Maybe you know of other ways to conserve energy.

The Three R's

Do you need help going green? Start by practicing the three R's. No, not **R**eading, w**R**iting, and a**R**ithmetic—but **R**educe, **R**euse, and **R**ecycle!

Reduce

- Reduce paper and plastic bag waste. Bring reusable canvas bags to the grocery store, use cloth napkins, and real plates.

- Bring your lunch to school in a lunch box-don't brown bag-it.

- Reduce the amount of water you use. Turn off the water while you brush your teeth. Only run the dishwasher and washing machine when they are full.

- Reduce the amount of electricity you use. Install new compact fluorescent light bulbs to save energy and money. Turn off and unplug appliances when they are not in use.

- Reduce air pollution and greenhouse gases by walking or riding a bike (it's good exercise too!). If that is not possible, try to share a ride or use public transportation.

Reuse

- Let someone else use your unused things. Donate items to charity, instead of throwing them out.

- Reuse plastic tubs and glass jars instead of buying new storage containers.

- Reuse organic food waste and yard waste by creating a compost pile.

Recycle

- Recycle paper, plastic, and metal items so they do not end up in landfills.

- Buy items made from recycled products.

- When you grow tired of your video games, books, and DVDs, get together with some friends and trade!

Glossary

agriculture (AG-ruh-KUL-chur): business of producing crops and raising animals

atmosphere (AT-muhs-fear): a mix of gases that surround a planet

efficient (uh-FISH-uhnt): working without wasting energy

ethanol (ETH-uh-nol): an alcohol fuel made from some grains, corn, and sugar cane

fossil fuels (FOSS-uhl-FYOO-uhl): coal, oil, and natural gas formed from plants and animals that lived millions of years ago

generator (JEN-uh-ray-ter): a machine that converts energy to electricity

industry (IN-dus-tree): manufacturing companies and other business

molten rock (MOHLT-uhn-rok): rock melted by heat

photosynthesis (FOE-toe-SIN-thuh-siss): a chemical process by which plants make their food

photovoltaic cells (FOE-toe-vol-TAY-ik-sellz): devices that can produce electricity when exposed to sunlight

reservoir (REZ-ur-vwar): large natural or manufactured area that holds water

thermal (THUR-muhl): having to do with heat

turbine (TUR-bine): an engine driven by air, water, steam, or gas

Index

Further Reading

Jakab, Cheryl. *Energy Use.* Black Rabbit Books, 2008.
Orme, Helen. *Energy for the Future.* Bearport Publishing, 2008.
Wheeler, Jill. *Renewable Fuels.* ABDO Publishing, 2007.

Websites to Visit

www.doe.gov/forstudentsandkids.htm
http://powerhousekids.com

About the Authors

David and Patricia Armentrout specialize in nonfiction children's books. They enjoy exploring different topics and have written about many subjects, including sports, animals, history, and people. David and Patricia love to spend their free time outdoors with their two boys and dog Max.